MW00329794

THE VICTORIA AND ALBERT COLOUR BOOKS

FIRST PUBLISHED IN GREAT BRITAIN BY
WEBB & BOWER (PUBLISHERS) LIMITED
9 COLLETON CRESCENT, EXETER, DEVON EX2 4BY
IN ASSOCIATION WITH THE VICTORIA AND ALBERT MUSEUM, LONDON

BOOK, COVER AND SLIP CASE DESIGN BY COOPER THIRKELL LIMITED

PRODUCTION BY NICK FACER

TYPESET IN GREAT BRITAIN BY THE VANTAGE GROUP

PRINTED AND BOUND IN HONG KONG BY
MANDARIN OFFSET INTERNATIONAL LIMITED

BRITISH LIBRARY CATALOGUING IN PUBLICATION DATA

ROCOCO SILKS—(THE VICTORIA & ALBERT COLOUR BOOKS; 1)
1. DECORATION AND ORNAMENT, ROCOCO 2. SILK
1. SAUNDERS, GILL II SERIES
746'.0439 NK1355

ISBN 0-86350-084-6

THE VICTORIA AND ALBERT COLOUR BOOKS

ROCOCO SILKS

WEBB & BOWER

MCMLXXXV

IN 1978 the Victoria & Albert Museum acquired an album containing 223 designs for printed textiles. These watercolour drawings are the only extant evidence we have of William Kilburn's activities as a designer, yet they more than justify his reputation. Unfortunately no existing textiles can be attributed to him with any certainty, though the Dictionary of National Biography tells us that 'the beauty of his designs established him as one of the most eminent calico-printers in Europe'. Contemporary sources suport this judgement, to the extent that James Thompson of Clitheroe, giving evidence before the select committee on the 'Present State of Manufacturer . . .', 1833, could declare that 'Raymond, Kilburn, Wagner and Edwards are regarded as the old Masters of the English school of design in calico-printing'.

William Kilburn (1745-1818) was born in Dublin, the son of an architect. He was apprenticed to Jonathan Sisson, the owner of a linen and cotton printing factory at Lucan, eight miles outside Dublin. Much of his spare time was devoted to drawing and engraving, devising patterns for chintzes, and copying the designs of others for his employer. When his apprenticeship ended he moved to London and settled in Bermondsey; here he earned a living by selling his designs to calico printers (London and its environs being at that time the centre of the industry). He also became acquainted with a near neighbour, the botanist William Curtis. Impressed by his draughtsmanship Curtis employed him to produce some of the plates for his *Flora Londinensis* (1777-87), A number of plates in the first edition are fully signed by Kilburn or bear his initials, and the work is of a high standard, finely executed and botanically exact. But the textile industry offered more lucrative employment and he accepted a position as manager of a calico-printing factory at Wallington in Surrey. After seven years he was wealthy enough to purchase the factory outright. Much of his success and repute was undoubtedly due to the quality and originality of his designs. His pieces of muslin chintz, with their exquisite detail, sold for a guinea a yard; he presented one of them (a seaweed pattern) to Queen Charlotte. Of course these beautiful but expensive fabrics were much copied, and Kilburn suffered grievously from plagiarism, cheaper imitations were printed and marketed within ten days of the originals appearing at Brown, Rogers & Co., the wholesale linen drapers in Cheapside who were the proprietors of most of Kilburn's designs.

In 1787, therefore, Kilburn led a group of manufacturers in petitioning Parliament with complaints of the severe losses they suffered as a result of the many 'base and mean Copies' of their 'new and elegant Patterns'. They sought some legal protection similar to the copyright enjoyed by authors and engravers. Kilburn was called before the committee of inquiry to prove these allegations; he declared that his patterns, if popular, were 'immediately copied upon Coarser Cloth and in bad Colours' so that in three years he had lost a thousand pounds' worth of prints a year through imitations. As evidence he produced 'an original Pattern upon British Callicoe paying a high Duty, of his own Design, and also a Counterfeit of the same in coarser Cloth, paying a lower duty'.

The immediate result of this petition was a bill, passed in May 1787, as 'An Act for the Encouragement of the Arts of designing and printing Linens, Cottons, Callicoes and Muslins, by investing the Properties thereof in the Designers, Printers and Proprietors for a limited Time' (two months, in fact). The act seems to have worked well, and was renewed in 1784 on receipt of a second petition from Kilburn and others requesting an extension of the time limit to three months. It could not, however, arrest the decline in the London trade as competition from Lancashire increased. The London companies foundered, and Kilburn himself was declared bankrupt in April 1802.

Kilburn's designs would have been block-printed. This had been the basic technique since the art of calico-printing came to Europe from India in the 1680's. Around 1760 it was superceded by copperplate printing which allowed larger repeats and more finely detailed impressions. But by the 1790's the standard of block-cutting had improved considerably, and by hammering thin copper strips and pins into the block the printers were able to achieve an unparalleled fineness of line and detail. The major advantage of block-printing was that it allowed printers to use several colours; with rare exceptions the plate-printed cottons were monochrome – purple, red or indigo-blue on white – because of the problems of registration when printing from more than one plate. New dyes, including a fast yellow, were developed in the last decades of the 18th century, thus allowing the designer more creative scope with a richer palette,

Fine detail and rich yet subtle colour were the hallmarks of Kilburn's designs; most contemporary designs appear crude by comparison. Charles O'Brien, in his book *The British Manufacturers Companion and Calico-Printers Assistant* (1792) described Kilburn's patterns as 'perhaps the nearest approaches to nature in drawing'. Kilburn himself defined an original pattern as an 'Assemblage of Flowers or Fruits placed in a variety of Colours, so that they shall strike the Trade as something new, and not seen before', and all the designs in this album use floral motifs, accessorized with leaves, shells, ribbons or architectural elements. Kilburn demonstrates great skill in pattern-making, disguising the repeat successfully in both complex and simple designs. The flowers and plants are for the most part executed in a naturalistic fashion, though identifiable species are freely mixed with fantastic inventions, and the commonplace mixed with the exotic. The drawings show a familiarity with plant form and structure, evidence of his training in botanical illustration. Sometimes he allowed the plant structure to suggest the pattern; climbing or trailing plants such as convolvulus, bramble or common retch lend themselves perfectly to the demands of a delicate meandering pattern. Other plants may appear complete with roots to create a border, or to add feathery detail. A wide variety of garden plants and wild flowers are to be found in these plates; the identifiable species include roses and daffodils, narcissus, jasmine, bluebell, iris, lily-of-the-valley, pelargonium, and even a cactus (probably the hybrid *aporocactus flagelliforum*).

Though inventive and highly original Kilburn's drawings can be divided into categories which approximate to the successive fashions in chintz design. With the aid of dated pattern books, and the evidence of contemporary commentators it is possible to date particular styles with some precision. For Kilburn's album we also have definite dates, from 1788 to 1792, inscribed on the back of some of the drawings, and stylistic evidence suggests that this is an accurate date for the whole thing.

The largest group of designs are the floral arabesques and trails on a white ground, a style which derived ultimately from English silk designs of the 1740's and 1750's. According to Godfrey Smith (in *The Laboratory, or School of Arts,* 1756) the 'patterns for the callico-printers . . . are for the generality in imitation of the fashions of the flowered silk-manufactory' with 'natural flowers, stalks and leafs, sometimes intermixt with ornaments after the French taste; sometimes in sprigs and branches . . . dispersed in a natural and agreeable manner'. Kilburn produced a great many variations on this theme, ranging from the spare and delicate to the robust and luxuriant. Ribbons, a popular feature in Rococo silk designs, he replaced with the striped ribbon-like leaves of an ornamental grass, sometimes even representing them tied in knots and bows. The simplest patterns of this type are those in which single sprigs or small bunches of flowers are scattered over a white or pastel-coloured ground.

Kilburn's most original and delicate designs are those which employ a seaweed motif. Charles O'Brien, an invaluable guide to the changing fashions in chintz, makes a specific reference to Kilburn stating that 'His patterns for 1790 run chiefly on an imitation of seaweed, and in effect, at least, excelled what any other printer exhibited'. The seaweed is variously employed, either to create an 'all-over' pattern with or without scattered flowers, or bunched with other plants. The fine tracery of the seaweed is varied with corals, mosses, or skeleton leaves. Another invention of his own are the textured grounds of curling leaves or twisting stems which provide a foil for brightly coloured flowers.

The seaweed patterns also occur on black or coloured grounds. 'Dark-ground' floral chintzes enjoyed a vogue in the last decade of the 18th century, both for dress and for furnishings, and Kilburn includes a number

of dark-ground designs. Again O'Brien refers to 'dark or shady patterns (according to the present humour)' and also to 'a late imitation of a dark ground pattern, with a kind of moss or spray hanging down in great quantities'. Independent evidence from another pattern book establishes the dates for this particular style as 1790 to 1794. These dark-ground designs, which ranged from black through to plum, were densely patterned and often highlighted with white flowers such as jasmine. The dark ground itself continued in favour until 1800.

Striped patterns were also popular in the late 18th century but Kilburn's examples of this type are among his less attractive designs, smaller in scale and less detailed. In marked contrast are the borders and large-scale stripe designs; bold and brilliantly coloured they incorporate architectural elements and sea-shells. They anticipate the florid styles of mid-Victorian decoration and must surely have been intended as furnishing fabrics.

As beautiful as these drawings are something of their subtlety must have been lost in the process of cutting and printing; even so Kilburn excelled his rivals and imitators to achieve, as O'Brien said, 'the nearest approaches to nature . . . as far as cutting would allow, and in colour as far as three reds, three purples, buffs, olaves, and so on would permit'. It was Kilburn's triumph over such technical limitations that established his 'Old Master' status in the world of calico-printing.

THE PLATES

13

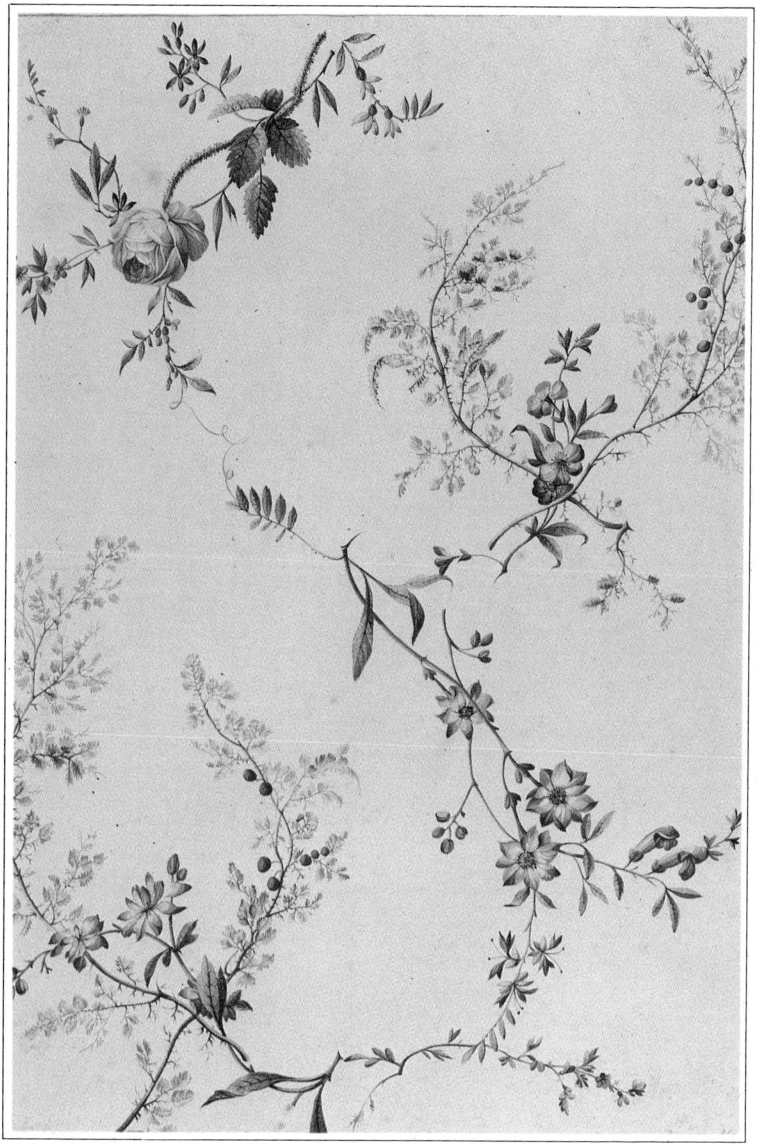

15

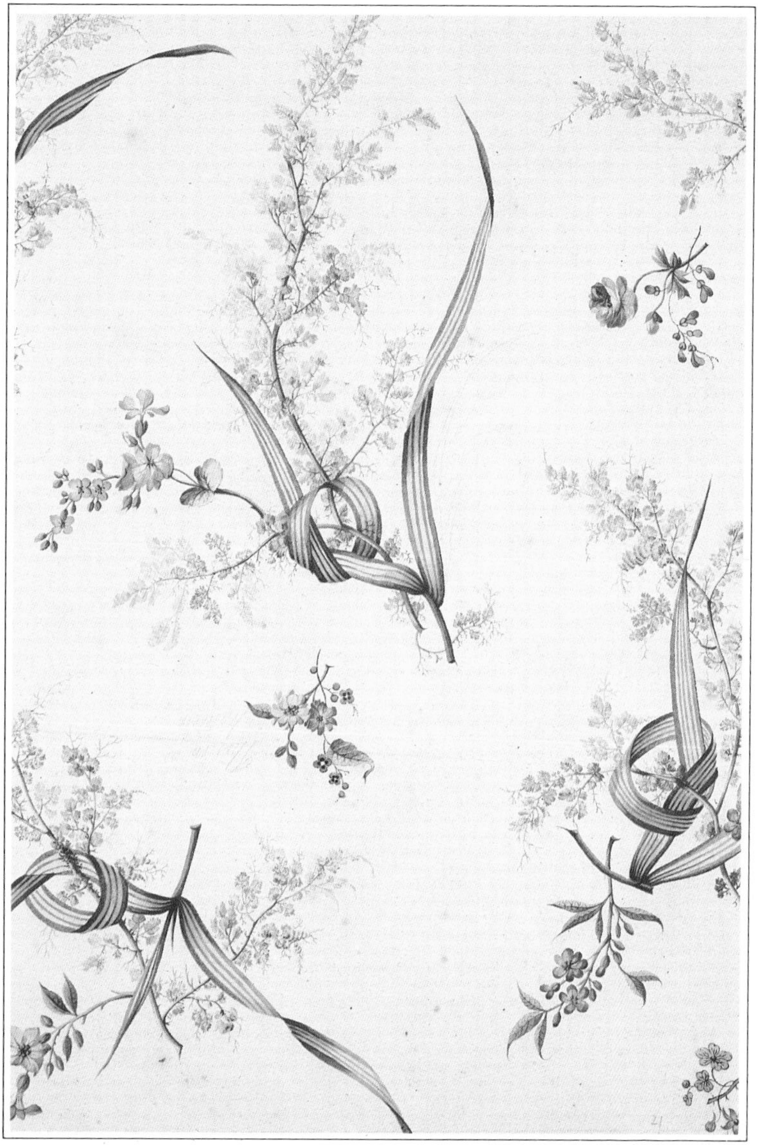

17

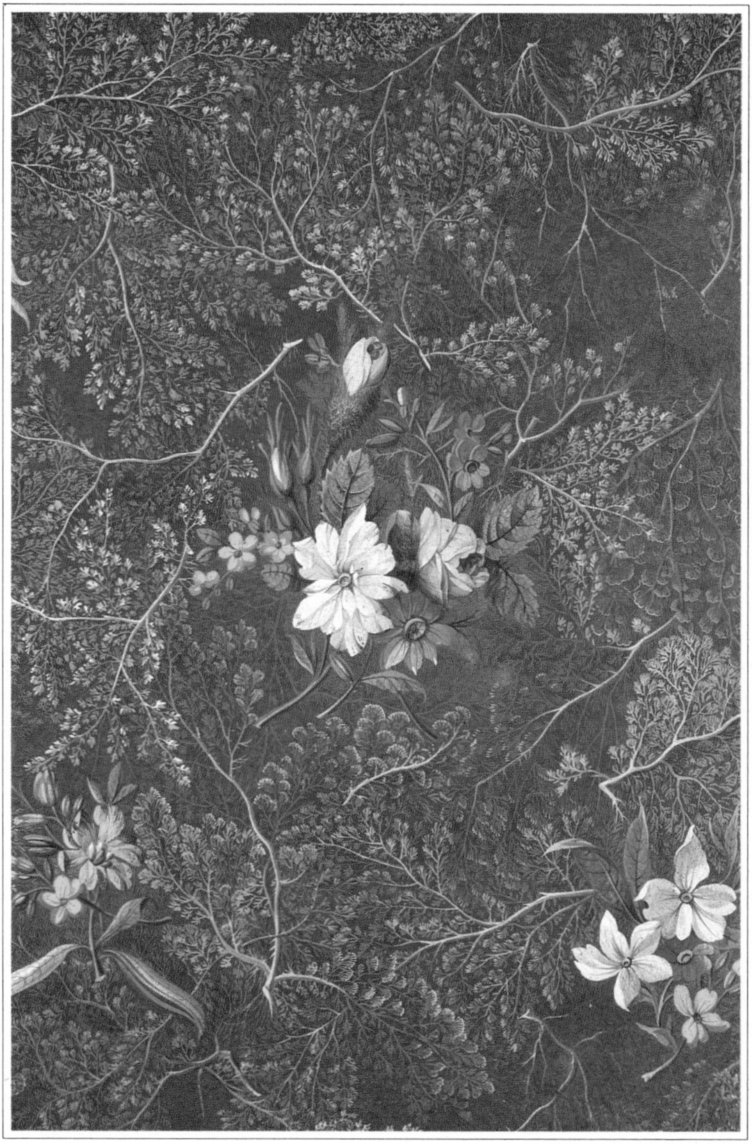

19

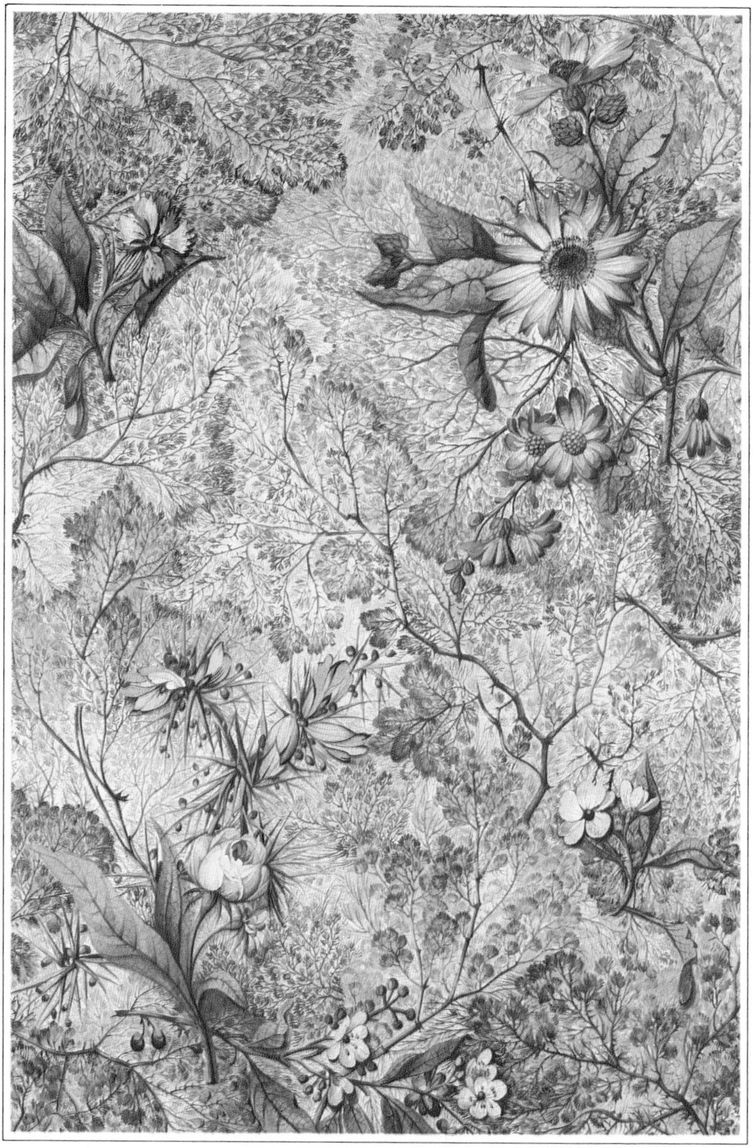

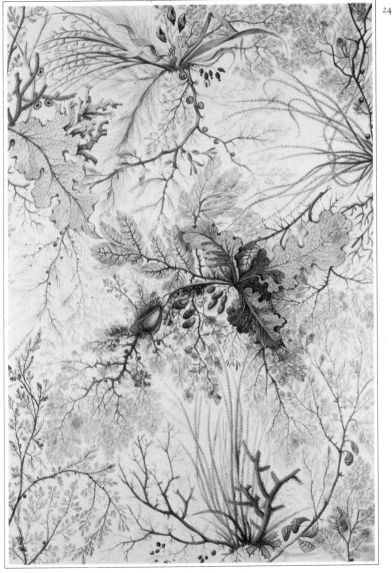

27

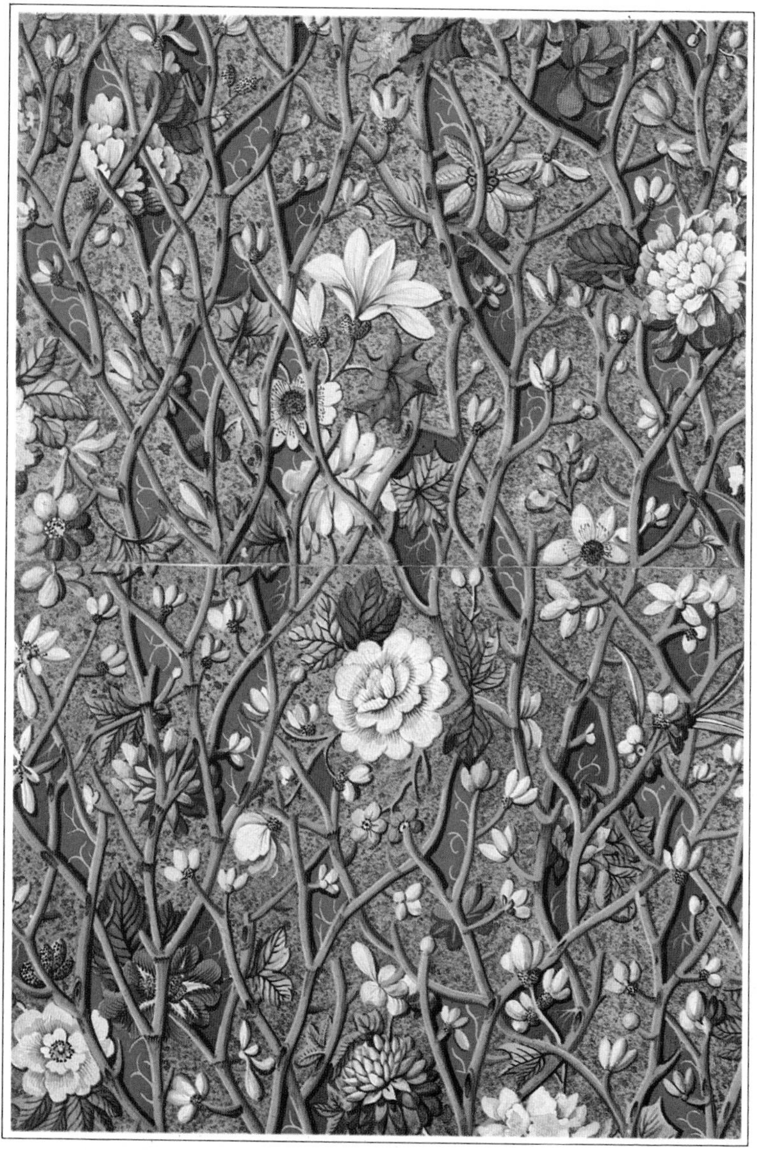

31

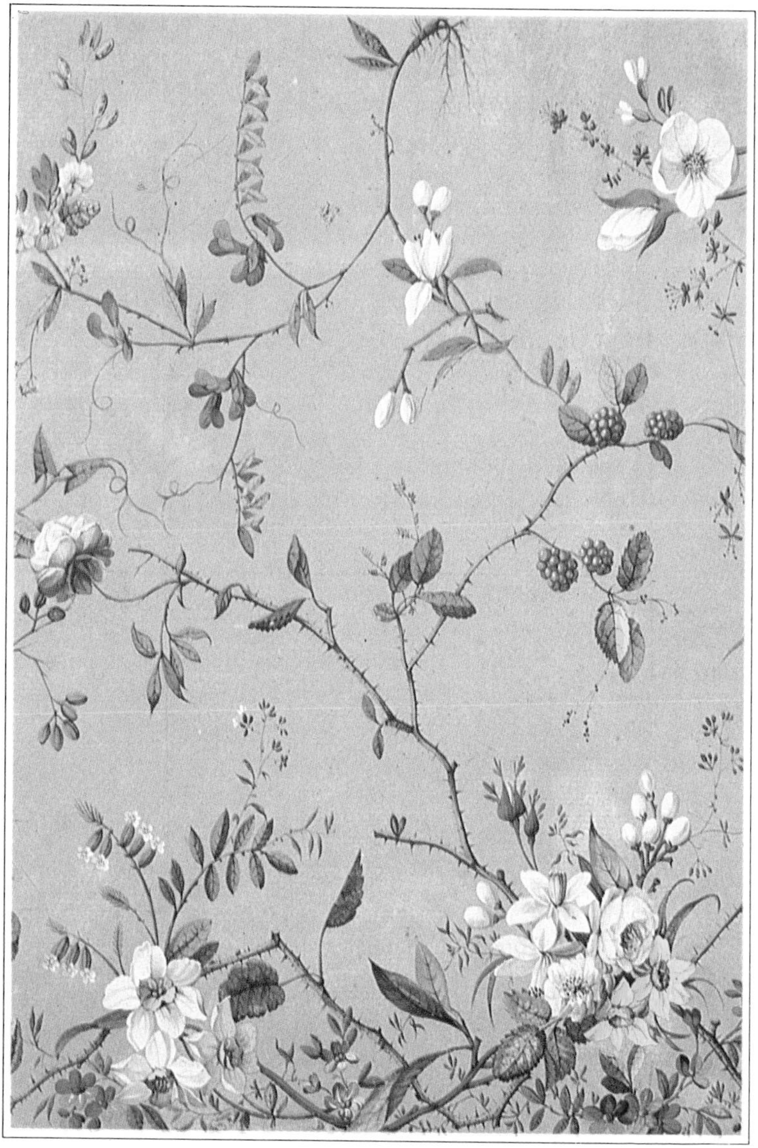

33

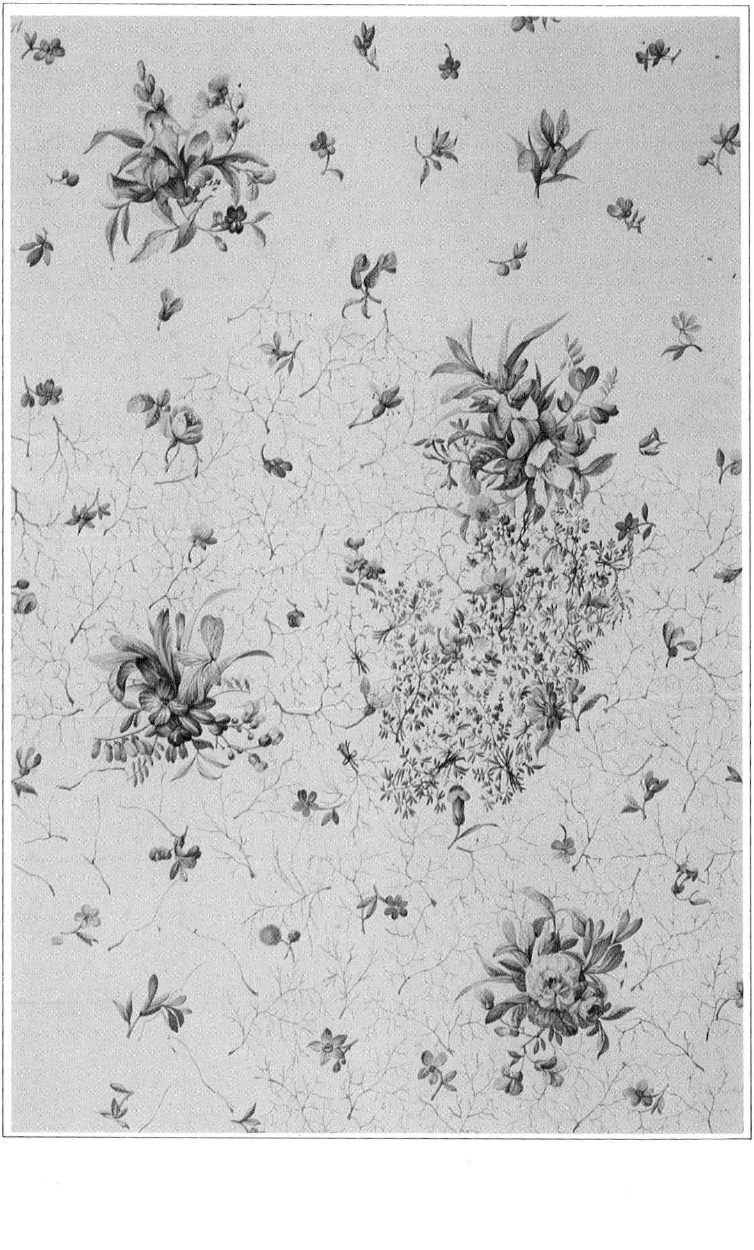